HERE

MAXINE CHERNOFF

HERE

Counterpath
Denver
2014

Counterpath
Denver, Colorado
www.counterpathpress.org

Poems have appeared in *Colorado Review, Volt, Laurel Review, Plume, Yew Journal, 99 Poems, Pebble Lake Review, Café Review, Drunken Boat, Interim, Puerto del Sol, New American Writing, Phoebe, Web Conjunctions, Conjunctions, Buenos Aires Review, Brooklyn Rail, Witness, Domestic Cherry, 14 Hills, Talisman, Star82 Review, As it Ought to Be, NOO Journal,* and the *NEA's Writers Corner.* A chapbook, *A House in Summer* (online edition), was published by Argotist Press, Liverpool. The author thanks all of the editors. The author also wishes to thank the NEA for a 2013 fellowship in poetry that aided in the completion of this manuscript.

Library of Congress Cataloging in Publication Data
Chernoff, Maxine.
[Poems. Selections]
Here / Maxine Chernoff.
pages cm
Includes bibliographical references.
ISBN 978-1-933996-40-0
I. Title.
PS3553.H356A6 2013
811'.54—dc23   2013016818

for you

CONTENTS

PART I

A House in Summer   3

Rune   5

Daphne   7

Construction   9

Commentary   11

Offerings   14

The Staggering Man   15

Gesture   16

Evidence   18

Anosognosia   20

Singular   22

Question   24

Heard   26

Parade   27

Notes   28

Aversions   29

Under the Music   31

Purchase   32

Atmosphere   33

Word   34

Drones   35

PART II

Stereopticon   39

Stereopticon   40

Stereopticon   41

Beheld   42

Window   43

Momentum   44

Again   45

"You starred in the movie . . . "   46

Knowing   47

Philosopher   48

Nocturnal   49

Road   50

There   51

Power   52

Song   53

History   54

Justice   55

Moment   57

Feature   58

"The path between us . . . "   60

Subplot   62

Edge   63

View   64

Literal   65

Letter   66

Here   67

Flight   68

Traced   69

Nature   70

"Out of nature . . . "   71

Legend   72

Sketch   73

Ascent   75

Later   76

"In certainty the self . . . "   78

Nest   79

Measuring   80

"Afternoon's bright awning . . . "   82

Gallery   83

For D.W.   85

Virginia Woolf wrote this paragraph.

—ERICH AUERBACH

In which a woman wonders when her son will grow taller, when the weather will clear and her husband stop throwing his negative shadow on clocks and lamps and objects as they are. Will it grow lighter despite his darkness, her eyes dry, though they are mostly dry, despite the feeling of tears welling up as she wishes for the boy to have more light.

Will the room, nature's repository of conical shells and tidy driftwood and small and radiant glass beads smoothed for centuries by water's vague intentions, have something to say about the figures that come and go, the careless boy, unhappy man and woman whose demeanor makes the room glow with the distinct light of sickrooms, though no one yet is ill—but there is the care and caution one associates with grief.

When shutters break loose and the wind does its work and the people who've shined with the moment's surprises and disappointments and failures to love quite well enough have left the room, will the wind acknowledge their vivid passing on sofas and loveseats where sand is ingrained in scalloped patterns of fabric woven to resemble teardrop-shaped leaves? Will photos teeter on walls in their dampened frames or simply be stacked in boxes for relatives to take to a coach house overlooking a stand of elms on a narrow hill that deflects the wind, where someday a woman opens the box in front of her grandson who asks without much concern, to pass the day, who were these people, did you know them?

And the woman, because she is sentimental but cautious with her emotions will say without conviction, I hear they were a family who summered at the beach, who lost their mother, who thought many things and then forgot them, who loved as well as they might, as I love you, she will tell her grandson, though not in words. She will think these words as he looks at her without knowing why her answer takes so long and when it does come seems to acknowledge some deep sorrow of inheritance neither can understand.

If this is in a book as most things turn out to be, the woman will have read it twice: once when she was young herself, a reader whose eyes grew teary for Mrs. Ramsey and all the love in the world that gathers in unmapped corners where someone comes to stand for no good reason, and then again when she is older and knows the pleasure of overhearing in her own voice things she might have said to calm herself and soothe a boy.

4

I am not what you supposed but far different.

—WALT WHITMAN

Not timber or bronze or iridium, not the old habits of species at a waterhole or the short irregular breaths
of the last whispered guest
Not the grievance that gives way to truth or the truth of a three-headed beast in your atlas of imaginary
travels
Not the speaker with the plans but the quiet boy learning the rope trick in the hallway outside the room
Not the intelligence noted for its acute air of judiciousness but the wasp's sharp sting as it strikes a shapely
passing ankle
Not the coiled answer waiting for its question unlike what is asked or required on a Sunday
Not the leaves in May shining ferocious in the garden where your grandson has left an onion resting on a
stone
Not the fierce attention of the man on the traffic island holding a sign that says something smeared by the
rain
Not the notice given by an eye to another in its hope of dependence on kindness or its hope of notice in a
room full of candles
Not the bored glance of a mother whose child has climbed higher than last time but is busy with hurt and
resentment
Not the author whose page is so filled with sound that he forgets each word's landscape is a story with
beginning and end

Not your hand or my hand or the things that we touch in a day which includes so many forms of heaviness, so much light

Not the tinge of memory in a place where someone else stood unaware of your life or its constant necessity to record its existence in each room's sharp corner

Not formal analysis or credo or code or the heard cries of pelicans over the water of the bay's dark shadow under the bridge

Not earth's solitude early in the day when most everyone is sleeping and you are alone in a kitchen where he or she once daily stood

Not the pouring of water or the boiling of kettles or the singing of neon as it advertises books or massages or bereavement services

Not Augustine of Hippo or Herodotus or Longinus or Mrs. Miller or Captain Courageous

Not the oldest book or rarest coin or smallest bird known to sip water from a clover

Not your face in a mirror or a window nor your voice as heard on a recording among the others nor your method of material witness to things as they open like a novel's first sentence

You are not in the room or the story or the thought you are not in the absence spoken as a charm against itself

> So much worse for the wood that finds it is a violin.
>
> —RIMBAUD

You try to find the easy answer to the question of the ages, the one that recedes as all steady dreams in a
   house of wakefulness.

You uncover a hasty truth, a candid lie, an answer like no other shaped like a boat with bat wings and
   certitude. This is no fable, no nursery rhyme. It is the trees' steady progress toward a cloud made of
   bones and abstract longing.

Nothing in its place, no place for facts rare as birth in a banyan tree during a flood—you saw the photo in
   the paper and imagined the woman who had climbed so heavily upward to preserve her story past harm.

Unlike Magritte's clever pipe or the oddly postured woman in the Balthus painting flung across a piano,
   you are serious as summer's crazy ripeness or winter's inevitability—a weedy patch without sun near the
   fence ignores both seasons.

You are a realist, saint of small remarks, hero of paper white as bone. You gesture to the moon or make
   a leap of faith. You honor the wood of things, the breath of things, the underlining in the script that
   doesn't know its own destination in the pageant of forgetting.

Forgotten, you say, to any object that offers its presence. Daphne grows so slowly you can't notice—all these years it's hidden behind other greening things. Hesitating nearby, you carve a space for apparition, a space for circumspection and regret. Without them you are nothing more than windows bracing for a storm.

Note: Pursued by Apollo, Daphne is transformed into a laurel (Laurus nobilis): "a heavy numbness seized her limbs, thin bark closed over her breast, her hair turned into leaves, her arms into branches, her feet so swift a moment ago stuck fast in slow-growing roots, her face was lost in the canopy. Only her shining beauty was left." Name of a rare, slowly maturing type of laurel plant.

Then the air was fully of wings, the doves came down out of the sunny blue like angels in a painting.
—WALLACE STEGNER

You try to build it with scarves and wigs, the hair of women from shrines in India cut for purity and sold for profit. You cut your nails, make sure you are clean enough, you take the scrupulous bath so you are ready for the Lourdes of chemicals, alcohol, tubes. This is the oblation, the vow not to outlast but to serve, to compensate as best you can for its eventual failure.

Bargains are different—you play tricks, crossing the road coolly in front of the barreling truck—let him dare rob you with an unplanned end. Punch lines abound—how she was hit by a garbage truck, a potato truck, at the side of a friend helping her shop that day—they were sharing an egg roll. You laugh outrageously but not with outrage when the impossibly beautiful movie does not end as it should but just accrues endings. No editor, no discipline—allegory of your life—everyone's too, this is general—so many scenes unlit, words mumbled on tape, false starts, abrupt curtailments.

You are making a collection of homely wisdom offered like cakes at the banquet. You are a snob about offerings—so much is trivial, small as an ant crawling with a large leaf bent leftward. The braveness, the unfairness, all the ways in Tibet and Peru and with eagles or crows they topple the body to provide something more substantial than your own grief for yourself, you, the best friend you've ever had, the one who knows your lies and quibbles and times you really really didn't mean it, you who had even outwitted yourself. How you'd delayed because there was something more tinged with promise, more warped by danger that drew you off course. You who threw away charts and itineraries and maps. You who said no and no thank you at best.

You have no menu. You have *this* with the cube for the day, the rectangle for the week, the larger square of the month that marks a time for flags, a day for fathers, a festival in a South Asian atoll, a calendar whose photo of mountains that seem celestial are merely granite and water condensed into snow. You have minutes of still being yourself, if shadow is you, if your hand holds a lime-green glass and takes a long sip you feel deep in your throat.

It's finally not about you but what others will say, what they whisper about the self that you weren't, all the same, really. You were quiet or self-composed, cheerful or foolishly so, alert till the end or unfeeling as ice. You are elsewhere, doubled, halved and zeroed. Maybe, you can report by letter or note or an oddly voiced message that you are with yourself elsewhere or nowhere, you have what you need. Not pinned to a board in a small room without windows or sewn on a jacket, not on a booklet with dates and a line and a face with your own flaming eyes and longish chin—no harm meant in the modesty of missing, in the simply lucid sense of being here but also unseen.

UR my service dog UR white graffiti in the white bathroom of the Snow King UR a man and a woman wearing leather at a funeral for a colonel in the Russian army UR one of us UR a gun in a church UR Allen Ginsberg so lonely that you write *Howl* and *Kaddish* because you have no one to love you UR listing UR sinking UR are a fly ball hit off the bat of someone in stripes Everyone wants to sleep with you UR in the army of a neutral nation a fake army that shoots fake bullets at birch

UR my mother in a crazy dress and an empty smile and stockings with seams UR my father in a car hitting the wall of a factory at 8 am on Thursday, October 17, 1974 LOL UR no one I know UR the last good wish I wished you (LOLLOLLOL) and then you were not there

UR the baby I had, three in all, the magic number that makes up the trinity of snack crackers the trinity of bones of saints the trinity of thesis synthesis trifecta I lost the race I lost the horse I watched the horse running so fast her hoof fell apart She was a great filly they said the horsemeat butcher was closed for summer Baudelaire's drainpipe was very beautiful The swan stole our baguette The park (according to the film we saw later) was full of prostitutes According to the film we saw later the initiation process must happen in Europe in World War Two and involve a slightly ugly and dim-witted boy who turns out to be funny and handsome and then dies Emily Dickinson's parking meter is set on out of time—truly you don't believe me please do She became a heroin addict and kept a pygmy rat in her room at college She became a nurse and killed sleeping patients with morphine She became the smooth hair of a sad woman in my class who plagiarized poems and reports and thought I didn't know She became my doe-eyed student who disappeared but not in body She became my mother with her vampire lips in the photo before the war She became a priest on holiday with dandruff and a penchant for escargots She became a Byzantine icon artist a pubic sculptor a little girl with one braid cut off by my friend in first grade She became a porn star who opened a restaurant in Northridge CA She became the only postmodern painting in Slocum Nevada She became the postscript to me she became me LOLLOLLOL

I am writing this knowing that it is first excessive and second unimportant I am writing this knowing that you may not approve of my sudden burst of prose at the end of a book of poems LOLLOLLOL which I used to think meant lots of love

Lots of love and BTW it means more, it means less, it means when you fly, I will try to join you in the vee-shaped clouds over the opera version of "Three Sisters" He says he saw a boring play with people talking I didn't understand it was "Three Sisters" who never leave and never stop talking until much later Trashy novels are the only ones that work It will not save you to write poems that save you I saw the girl to whom I once gave a B+ for not listening to me She deserved a better grade for not listening because she didn't listen so very well She was whole-hearted in her non-listening She broke the mold of non-listeners

If you were a cantaloupe, what would I be? If you were a mollusk, where would I sleep? If you were a tank, would I ride in your dark and steamy chamber?

Kings summon us and we come We are supplicants all in search of something to worship in a peculiar and profane way The Duke of Bavaria was an asshole he was worse than George Bush II maybe and maybe not LOLLOLLOL The king of Belgium thought his private factory was the Congo their trees his baubles You may lose life and limb if your mother has you in the wrong bed you may lose more if your mother has you with the wrong man we all lose everything eventually but the stories have different weight over time some are told and some are not some are redacted and blurred by water or tears or another liquid Where can I buy some fire? Where is the fire store in this mall? We do not know how to properly use things but use is of no use and value of no value My grandson eats worms and swears to their goodness It is protein I say we all need it daily My love is a white birch my love is a flower

Can you say the fucking name of the flower I ask her don't say those flowers with the white petals and the yellow center, say daisy, damn it, I tell her and she says that is elitist as is the word *imagery* Okay, let's call it vapor or if that is too abstract let's call it sidewalk Is sidewalk elitist? Is garbage elitist, or do you prefer the word *refuse*, which is easily misread Multiple readings, are they allowed here? Do I get to keep my marbles, my beautiful tiger's eye and turquoise the color of our planet? What must I surrender to get out of here? Do you need it all or just most? I will give you most without you asking I will give you all if I can LOLLOLLOL I have nothing and still have my integrity she said my justice he said my last word

It rained frogs in the movie. It rained cheddar cheese. It rained a big moon with a hole bitten through. How can you count it or sum it, the teacher once asked Say ask for a question not said Why were all teachers so sad in that building? Was it a sad building? Who drank the most, Mr. Larson or Miss Weatherbee, I swear that was her name She ran the Daniel Burnham speech contest which I lost when the bell rang and I forgot the rest of my speech like magic We were mean We were children We did not know

What is the sum of three gentlemen in a gondola? What is the sum of our natural inclinations toward deification of otherness? What is the sum of our woes? LOLLOLLOL

A cluster of belfries encants the human idea.

—RIMBAUD

The heart-shaped meteorite is not message or omen, talisman or cure.

Locket of the world's intention, correlation of tangent and bone:

The church in Bruges where the blood of Christ thickened in a vial is chained to a priest.

Death on vacation, a humid Sunday when he says something trifling,

then looks at her for the final time. Who notices that a train leaves unless it is bound for grief?

The man who said he'd been blinded but now could see had kept the knowledge of failing to himself.

His blue eyes told of the miracle, which meant he would keep reading Yeats to students who Twitter and
     text during his lectures, who read box scores and Google their names.

Heart from the sky, blood in the vial, fragments of what's said,

left over beauty on a train to Bruges become story by connecting the dots:

Words flee, wanting a home in another context. Let's build

a reliquary where, under indigo velvet and gilded lining, they can escape prying eyes.

A staggering man is carrying a salad across the street.

This is not the first line of a word problem about velocity or distance.

I am waiting for him to cross and we have locked eyes.

He is grimacing or smiling at me. I am smiling back.

This man has a disorder that makes his case singular. It has a name and prognosis.

He is one of a galaxy of staggering men whose provocation is unclear.

I have seen them stagger in other arenas, and I have ignored their staggering in moments of disregard.

The staggering man is finally across.

My pen is out of ink, and I am writing with a crayon I found inside the seat, turquoise I would say, but
    Indian blue its appellation, perhaps about the ocean.

I haven't written so many poems since my twentieth year when my professor said that he doubted a girl
    with my large intelligence but emotional restraint could write a single word

It sounds as if he was unkind, but his was a kindness to me, a mirror to hold up to my shadows.

The staggering man has receded.

The afternoon is brilliant with invented weather and sky-framing clouds. Several pigeons are harassing a
    dove, which one of my students has told me is just a smaller, dumber pigeon.

How are you today, my dear? Are you being viewed by someone who locks eyes with you and loves you?
    Have you read my parable and noticed its small devices?

Will you judge me with a deeper love than I could offer the staggerers and plaintiffs earlier in my years and
    see how I see your eyes in their reasons?

the fabric I ate / and ate.
—LISA FISHMAN

You are the one who lived beyond this and that, whose face was a recompense like a photo showing unknown people in a better time when snow covered most of the view they were trying to obscure, and smoke the rest, the beautiful variety of white smoke (maybe steam) with its waving tangents ascending to the cobalt dome of the sky.

You made televisions mad with war go blank or showed music that covered the news of more deaths here and certain lack of life there, you were with the white piano on fire and the candles blazing on the piano on fire, and on the lawn there were birds of various black hues with beaks cracking tiny yellow seeds, also there to distract you from the war.

You are the crack in the ceiling she noticed when he was not there, not in bed this night or that night, nor present in the morning. The curtains' breeze was static and the trees buzzed with peculiar light as she traced the sheets and shadows on walls and asked time to assist the process of slow forgetting which is similar to remembering but in muted, kneeling tones.

You are the record player for *my funny valentine* in this version and that version and some versions yet to be made by DJs who will break the song in half or quarters or sixteenths or forty-eighths and place parts of it elsewhere like leaves dried in books about the Moors and sing something else that reminds you of summer in Dallas or Prague or Vermont.

You are the locus of happiness locus of sorrow you are the water where dolphins nurse their young and the water that makes boats list in Williams' poem *The Yachts* which is not nearly his best with its driving rhythms and forced endings and endless triumphs—he is better on small projects as you are in making happiness a temporary patch in regard for the moment and nothing to follow.

You are the formlessness of form as it breaks from its song or shape or recent invention in independence from what surrounds it, the figure that goes from one shadow to the next without disputing its small place in the painting where men come and go and sell things packed on camels in a desert that reaches beyond the castle at the end of the Silk Road and the three subsequent left turns to the ancient widow's house.

You are the eventual practice of learning to wait by a pond as light changes from morning to day to generation to others at the same pond on a Saturday late in summer when she takes his hand and he breathes in deeply and tells her to come away from here, the edges are dangerous and far too filled with memory.

You are you turning back on yourself like a dress unsewn and unraveled and no longer quite cloth—more like paper—in a narrow closet where people leave things when they move and light slants as is its tradition in rooms that get lost in a story of leaves and seasons and long endings in patience-filled sunlight.

To philosophize is to learn how to die.
—MONTAIGNE

Of houses, empty or noticed, to rooms whose lamps have left their light behind, ancient after time has landed in the breech of its excess, dropped there as if a package fell from the arms of a woman.

Of glasses once filled whose essence is left in a stain that looks clear in most light but carries a tinge of its erasure when she notices it late in the night after he is asleep.

Of windows, whose eyes are shut to the diversions of their intended gazers, birds passing on their sheer migrations over oceans filled with brine.

Of gardens where he sat or she sat amid the trickery of a season and its aftermath, patchy on the lawn and patchy in the sky, gray and listless for a time before respecting the progress of feeling as it overtakes the geography of plants.

Of reasons which fill a space but not adequately, which stretch like deserts between needs vocalized or calmed, written or whispered, answered or forgotten by the time an answer is prepared.

Of books filled with language that is never proper to the moment but serves as a repository of the possible though the possible is not enough, as a tent is never enough in a storm.

Of eyes that fill with knowing or restless asking or a glance that means retreat or surrender or that a village lies in waste, a life is lost, small as a child's attempt to capture a mote of dust above his bed in moonlight from a gibbous moon.

Of melodies whose notes contain the promise of an answer, as if music is an answer or patience a virtue or love an antidote.

ANOSOGNOSIA

God knows where I am.
—LINDA BISHOP

Give up your princely crown: you never had it, your kingdom, your horses made of fire and tears. Give up your plans to sail the ocean in a vessel made of clouds and glue.

You are not you, not yourself, not the one whose whispers were heard by the teacher even when your lips were closed and your shiny boots on the ground. You are not the one heralded at the refuse dump by the seagulls whose cries were also the cries of a little girl dropped in a well.

You are not the handsome stranger who is awaited in the house where thirty-nine apples are rotting near the sink drain and the woman lies on the floor almost dialing a number in Connecticut of a relative whose hands were too large and too close.

Give up your jewels, the glass brooch in the shape of Siam, where you once ruled a gaggle of women who praised you in eight languages and shared your shadow with no one. Give up your heraldry and your whispered treasons by the site of the buildings that once stood as an outline even on coins.

You are not the child in the closet pretending to be the ghost of Julius Caesar. You are the lady on the bus in rags asking for pennies because she is building a ladder taller than a northern pine that will reach beyond her most feared cloudburst.

You are not the comfort of a room where she rocked and held her child before she heard it tell her that treason was in the air, that the room was filled with dirt, that a certain chief of state had it in for her unless she enunciated correctly and plainly on a certain Friday before Flag Day the names of all the ghosts and saints beginning with K.

Give up your plan to beat the dead at their game of cards, your plan to conquer Las Vegas with your lamè gown and tulle, your plan to grace the state dinner for the King of Nubia with your crown of gold thorns and thistles from your neighbor's yard.

You are not someone with a plan, you are a woman made of bone and lace, a woman made of iron and nakedness, a woman made of words and excuses for them, you are under their care, you are subject to a plan that will enable you to be among them, to gather stars if you wish but keep them secret.

Anosognosia: patients in denial of their own disorders and thus refusing treatment for them, as in the case of schizophrenia.

Death's outlet song of life . . .
—WHITMAN

Every man should be so much an artist that he could report in conversation what had befallen him.
—EMERSON

High-mindedness is a construct of mind and its metals, its iron and zinc, its blue mercury.

It is a waste to consider how we relate to the human condition—we are the human condition in cotton and lace and charms that fit in thimbles. We are broken and fixed. We are mended and torn. We are the underlining of the soft belly of kangaroos crossed with examination books. We tell jokes that aren't funny and laugh with our eyes closed. When we open them, someone has died and another been born.

We praise Jove. We praise Allah. We praise the mark-downs at the Nordstrom Rack where a handsome young woman was weeping into her hands. We praise the immaterial essence of clouds that resemble your uncle on Wednesday. We praise the material grace of your hand on my collarbone, soft in its landing there.

We are unkind to our neighbors. We cheat on our friends. We are witnesses to the first bee in the jasmine we planted at noon. We are witnesses to the harms of a life and its slow repetitions that lead to new beauty. We travel to see peasants enact old rituals that we would find foolish in our own doorways. We are peasants as well under our skirts and children and finally fools. Who knows the height of a well-built arch or the dimensions for travel to Mars? They say if you fly there, you cannot return. There are those who will fly there. I heard them on a show discuss how they'll grieve for irises and children and the small fond expressions of those whom they love.

We all leave cathedrals and ashes and bony candles burnt to their wicks. We all leave nothing we wanted and everything we did and that of an in-between state of a small conversation involving the beauty of spires.

We are not jugglers. Planes fall and leaves too and nothing that crashes or lands without sound gets repaired. Our ankles have sight of the horizon of small endings. We look forward to more as we leave more behind.

When my mother was dying, she asked, "Will I live?" I remember the silence as she turned from our silence to make herself ready, the quiet of an afternoon in a room where light and sound were present but respectful. I remember the quiet later that day as we stood alone with her. Absent at last, she withdrew with a tact saved for endings.

Please save me from all that I know must follow. Please give me a book or a song or a look that means less.

QUESTION

a dream hesitates, it doesn't ask

—FANNY HOWE

you ask   and it's given
ten fingers   hands' rotation   dusty rings of planets
saints who died thinking   of ten states of bliss

you ask   and it's given
the cobalt message bottle   those who wandered green and bitter
in the cobbled desert   (the Bedouins all have cell phones, my son explains, their sons listen
to Michael Jackson)   we do not want things to change   but they do

you ask   and it's given
the perfect text   words of bird throat and hummingbird tongue
words of dolphin in shafts of comparable light

you ask   and it's given
tragic lady on the stairs whose hat flew off   would Godard have liked
our mad dash   (we were always in films without asking)

you ask and it's given
the irresistible sky   the sky over us   separately   and together   we hear of bombs
in another world   (our world)   the one that cracks so easily   that allows in
the sweet with the bitter

you ask and it's given
the calm   the storm   the death   the waking   the asking

Error, errancy, and bewilderment are the main forces that signal a story.

—FANNY HOWE

You are a rough draft
Lost in a dream of salt flats of words on paper
You are melting in fog
You are lifting off the page like a flock of swallows
You are the grass tangled in life without permission
Green as a pledge or a warning
You are the evidence of snow evidence of daylight before you remembered its name
You are a measure of progress which of course has ended, which happened before you
You know what to call it—you call it something else
Maybe *limit* or *reservoir* you are spilling into your own accord
With seasons with particulars with eventualities that mean nothing
You know that to reproduce a figure you must learn to see its contraction
You must steadily approach a shadow without altering its borders
You must cut a shape from a shape inside of nothing
You must practice forgetting until it is science
You are an ornament of nature a gesture of surrender
To words you once recognized as your own

The laughter of those missing/makes it clear . . .

—BEI DAO

Is it the beginning or end of the story when the road turns southward into nothing and a coyote is seen on a hillside above the tract houses and the fund-raising march approaches the house where she died last night quite late after a short illness?

She is no longer there, cushioned in moonlight, no longer a prime number, proof of her son's voice when he called for comfort the day he discovered his heart could break.

Not present for endless war and sorrow, which she will happily miss, not in the audience but in a solitary role she would mock were she asked. Who asks? Who speaks of her in the garden of the neighbor she barely knew who has become responsible for mortality as it relates to their cul-de-sac?

The neighbor's husband knows it uplifts her to care about strangers, contains her as the uncontainable leaks from the television into their ears. He remembers *The Enormous Radio,* from which Cheever's protagonist hears all the tawdriness of strangers. He has learned to console her anonymous grief far better than her inventory of harms, mostly related to him.

The fund-raisers wear pink. A hideous parade outside his window. The new widower hears a megaphone tell the group of women and a few sad men that every step helps the living remember.

Her death is excluded, her death like scrimshaw, rare carving in ivory, he thinks, souvenir of vanished time that won't hold value. Is the daytime moon in a phase he's never noticed, white and jagged as a paper cut?

Find the mortal world enough.
—W.H. AUDEN

Light's history intrudes on the sentence at midnight. A thought enters like an asterisk over the word *ocean*.

You are witnessed from the inside, your blood discoursing with itself over ethics and science.

It's the same you draped in the crease of a flag or over the moon, lost in the footage of newsreels with your bobbed hair and inevitable luster of a different era.

On the wall near the accustomed view, your hand is silhouette. The image arrives without its reasons, a stone's throw away from remembering.

In the summer house near the pier, nothing crashes except vagueness and circumstance.

The last train leaves its station without analysis. You've seen it before in a film, the present recognized from its legend.

All endings are preludes—the evil man came to harm before the story cast its light on the screen you watched with worry and regard.

You tie one end of your question to the other. The answer lapses into knowing and sundering, one cloth sewn as the other is ripped.

Pray Heaven that the inside of my mind may not be exposed.

—VIRGINIA WOOLF

An aversion to Viennese music, the type she heard in her youth at the great amusement park by the dying green river, where all the swallows nested nearly on top of one another under a bridge and scared her with their dense blackness. Why it was the pipes of the organ that frightened her more she was unsure; perhaps the brash and hollow sound of the low notes felt oddly like wind in a desert though she had never been to a desert—or cold touching her skin at night as she changed positions in her child's narrow bed.

He was terrified of bees in any form, forms of honey, the names would throw him into a panic; clover honey, Tupelo honey, pine, whipped or combed. Who whipped or combed it, he wondered. And the bees' regurgitation of the nectar, the stickiness of the product, as if one could get oneself entangled finger by finger in its goldenness. As to seeing the bee itself, he would wait until dark to take walks to a bench under the elders where he'd read books on Vikings and space aliens, who had nothing to say about honey.

Her fear of cloth made it very hard for her to concentrate at the shirt factory. The bright fibers gleamed, the stripes a sin in themselves of color and pattern and roads she had forgotten to take when she'd left him. One would have brought her to a different city where she could have worked as a maid, perhaps, but then there'd be laundry and sheets; or maybe as a baker, but the flour would get sifted and poured and rolled into a perfect rectangle of significance, nearly substantial as cloth. Anything but the hum of the sewing machine on her table and the one next to hers, where the girl with the extra finger sewed even more slowly than she and whistled as he did, a melodic low tone like the kettle beginning to boil the morning she had left him for good.

His first memory of his mother's arms couldn't have been at so early an age as he imagined. Most sources say one's true memories don't exist before kindergarten. But he knew he had seen her look away when she gave him the bottle, her sunlit blue eyes blank as water. She wanted to be elsewhere, he realized, and thought for her of places that would have easily outdone the holding of this small bag of bones—what a skinny, unattractive baby, people had said, thus the supplemental bottles of a mixture of pure cream and goat's milk. He dreamed they sailed off together in a little white boat on a vast calm sheet of blue sky, he and his mother floating out of reach of the doctors and nurses and allusions to his failure to thrive that had made her so sad and unconfident.

Together they hated any type of berry. Summer was worst when the stores filled with the patriotic colors of the fruit, their reds and blues, their small variation from Sweden, the lingonberries of Ingmar Bergman, the gooseberries of Chekhov, orbs and dents and pure circularity. Neither was allergic—they concluded that the first time they met at a picnic where they sat like sad leftovers next to a plate of creamed corn. On Thanksgiving they made the usual feast, but they were so in love they barely ate—the turkey they had roasted for so long sat on the table looking as it had been buffed to brightness. While in bed in a blissful tangle of ankles and thighs and arms, what they thought most about was their delight in having excluded cranberries from their plates. By spring it was over. The stirring they'd felt that summer in the berry aisle amid the lushness flown in from three countries on two continents was now a steely indifference, an aversion to one another, as if even a touch might elicit a cry of pain or a reverse of joy so sharp it would cut them. One night she almost ate a strawberry to declare independence from him but refrained at the last second.

Under the music, a baby cries in the audience. A police siren meets a thunderclap meets quantum theory.

Under the music you are falling into a sleep so calm that your face becomes architecture, your head and arms a latitude. Knees bend, and you breathe an intelligence heard in the room's soft air.

It is May here, the third month of spring. Already flowers die and new ones approach life, prodigious in their powers. Tendrils reach from under fences. Hands touch.

We build fences and sandbag rivers. We launch drones that fly crookedly toward their targets, launched by boys one might have taught bead work at scout camp.

You stand there, lovely in your harmlessness, gazing at a neighbor's fence, where a Stellar jay rips at a tissue. New jasmine twines over older vines. Nothing can stop it, not even your concern for its reaching.

You think it's a dream that you chop down trees in a vacant room, part of a house whose roof is treetops. Lilies overtake the more famous flowers. Is it life when flies buzz over blurred leaves? Words prefer the color of bees.

Is it a painting when the night swirls close and you hear the beaks and tongues of birds at your neighbor's pond where an egret perches on a stone eating koi?

You are water frozen and unlabeled. What you leave of yourself gets remembered as the wobble, stare, or remnant when you turn to look and touch his skin in the blue room softened by spring.

Kindness is amplitude of attention, always the distance of reason and retort as intention dims. Vermeer's corners, famous for their absence of color, shine like a lamp in your favorite midnight room. Figure and ground seized by attention—what you want is *here* and *here*.

One practical gesture leads to another. A hand closes. An eye sees the fraying darkness and its cover of recognition.

That which one ceases to be no longer exists.

—MONTAIGNE

Rain pummels windows, words unshake trees.

I have not looked outside all night.

As if distance were merely a loose wire. We are talking, nowhere but here and here, my love.

I do not doubt your existence—any more than I can walk on the ocean floor (nonchalantly as a ghost).

Shut in winter's house, not epic's dark gray, trees without corollary, a small flame wavering as shadows burn and waver.

Something expert closes a gap in curtains. I'll repeat, then you: this gaping vault we'll fill with clocks and days and numbers. There is only time.

You are offered a window or widow, a Coptic stance, a bed of lightning, angels scarred by conclusions. All that escapes is matter seeking matter seeking redemption.

Under the cover of lawns in summer, angels scarred with conclusions, a hum of parasols from the pointillist past when the world was picnic and soft intention.

You are left to marshal the parade, to transcribe the waves when they encounter a body or driftwood resembling her face.

A trance envelops the flagpole, a layer of mist sinks under the headlights as they race toward a desert where a filament of reason perhaps lies under a stone.

Don't breathe a name under cover of winter stars. Don't witness the opening of grace as it descends on the two who sit calmly by the lake.

You are not yourself as a stone is itself, as a match has potential, as an idiosyncrasy contains the necessary crease in the story.

The story exists for you alone. It is not your raft or transparency, carpet or dome.

In a place you once stood, water finds its level and trails off into a sentence.

Operators fly the planes from air-conditioned trailers thousands of miles from the war zone.

Porch lights appear—it is 1962 when the woman wearing a pink chemise retrieves the newspaper from her lawn.

We settle on news of our day, how video-games have turned deadly, how children have learned the ready skills of removal.

A book's pages blow from middle to end to beginning. Nothing passes or ends. Nothing claims the text's attention. Words float upward, launched by hands.

The usual mixed with the strange is the stuff of dreams, the stuff of waking to distinctions sharp as paper, soft as candles. Far beyond shadows, a light whose origin is mystery; a new sense of the word means death, sudden as music.

Maps suggest the land has no boundaries, countries no borders. Objects of interest move on a grid: men and women, cattle, and a stray goat with stone-colored eyes.

The ache of the past connects to the present—how doorbells used to ring and strangers call. Fear was small and hovered on lips. Olives floated listlessly in drinks as people whispered local scandal in front rooms blue with information.

Surgeons of excision, men enact death's plans. Its subtlety knows no limits; out-manned and outmaneuvered, we practice remembering.

From the outside, I suppose I look like an unoccupied house.

—WALLACE STEGNER

No one questions the future's glass bowl seers, the chemical air of sorrow or whorl of plastic forming the ocean of scraps. Noisy birds witness a day familiar or vague, crisp as a leaf or filled with slate-roofed clouds. Someone says disaster. Another cries mercy as prayers are balanced on pillows. The tragic comes to pass signaled by continual construction, by dead bees in autumn, by "answering the letter means I am lost, love," in reference to the almond trees near the gate where he stood among dappled gardens near a trellis that leaned like a private idea. Rowboats like slippers filled the harbor on a Sunday, and a small man waved from a perch on the pier, his flags and whistles tied to a board next to the sign for ultimate cures. The woman seated in the wagon felt air on her hands. A horse observed a moth pass under the arch in the square. Her small basket was dropped and fingers retrieved her beads, grace near an orchid and stone carved with numbers. He was holding a book when the ninetieth day of summer passed without remark, when the tiny globe on the three-legged stool shook, its world underwater, just as dust floated over darkly-etched branches.

Rowboats like slippers fill the harbor. Lights bob like lemons on water. The ninetieth day of summer passes without remark. Under the sign for ultimate cures, amber bottles with dry, suspicious corks balance on a shiny plank. Near a trellis that leans like a private idea, he pauses by the almond trees teeming with bees and finds a stick whose underside reveals decay in the greenness of August. His future holds no promise. He lays down his book of curious beasts. He likes the snake-headed woman whose shoulders are bare, except for a shawl, having found such wonders in a market thick with sugar and scarves, honey and dates, hills of coins and blue glass charms near a stone wall made in a war. He prefers evening in its hopeful shadows when old men get lost in thought. On such a night, he had first seen her in a wagon near a hexagonal marker. It seemed her arms were filled with air.

She examines the tiny globe, world underwater, and writes slowly, "Answering this letter means I am lost, love." Dark boughs of a tree hit the side window. She imagines a rustling in all of nature, wind swarming the trellised gate where he stood among the almonds trees blossoming. He had shown her the picture of the snake-headed woman with delicate, smooth arms. He collected amber bottles from the market that summer, poison vials, he called them. He had never hoped. If bees sent him solace, if love were a cure. She found comfort in a blue door frame surrounded by the dark, ancient ivy of novels. Soon it would be winter, the harbor frozen, fish like embers under ice. *Ultimate cures,* a slogan on the pier, a trick of summer when amber shined in a window to decorate an hour.

. . . gives to airy nothing
A local habitation and a name.
—THESEUS, "A MIDSUMMER NIGHT'S DREAM"

Let us be imagined by the sympathetic eye, borders realigning, singularity lost as bees in cumulus clouds over a locus of belief. To stare at the world, thinking it fragile despite root systems deep and undismissable. To be dust under a stairwell or a book left open as one sleeps. To comfort the view and conjure grace, blessing a glass of water or a hand that finds a small, sheer ledge that yields to remembering.

The actual knocks on any closed door, beggar's robe tattered, features obscured in the dark. Light clarifies an edge of knowing, secret theme left as a match near a candle. Nothing that touches another close object can keep itself whole—dust meets shadow, inscribing an arc. Dominions are small, crevice or crease in a story, parenthesis of an hour. The amaryllis grows in a day, its solstice private and ancient, flowering into the told.

Anyone accumulates a downfall.

No stranger to call or response, you wander in velocity's style through syllables of grace.
You are accustomed to fact as lie, lie as truth, encumbered beyond a sight of landing.
Under your costume you are woman whose hair was cut short last year and remained that way.
You are her voice under her own, her taste of certain minerals harsh to the ear of promise.
Promise to waste warmth on geography, volatile intention to burn the woods, its features and maps.
Mistake's knowing face set boundaries for your own—you come in love, leave in resemblance.

You ride upon trestles to dream's remembered peak, where you exchange words for sentence, meaning's unholy cargo of wished endings and lofty songs. Toward the known birds of late afternoon, toward the uncertain plane of reason beyond the turn in your thoughts of brokenness or hope, there you are with your silence and breath. In a room in the house of language, you drop intention's offered theory and claim a minute's circumstance, alone at the table where apple is round and pear fulfillment.

You starred in the movie with Maud Gonne and Socrates and Juliet and a flock of sparrows that were a fixed point like the spire of a cathedral but made of feathers. You were naked and clothed and wearing nothing visible except when you sat or stood or began to speak, and then the words were made of black yarn, and your fingers held them as in an outline of reverie. You were there and not there and when I partially held you, the idea of you faded into a hint of light tinged by a window in the westernmost sky. And under the window, your face was vaguer and therefore more intimate in its shadowed complexity. If water is proof of thirst and knowledge a satisfied hour with a book, then stories end as they begin at the height of invention without a suffix of time and its pressures. You starred in the movie, and certain necessities fled like figures animated by their own recognition.

A secret dream of emulating the cartographer or the diamond cutter animates the historical enterprise.

—PAUL RICOEUR

You're here on a couch, pillows fluffed, dreaming in Latin. You're in a tablet carved on a mountain and given to men whose ears filled with ontology. You're near a stream whose source is the next cogency for a traveler stunned as Hölderlin trying to remember his name. You're in the dream in which his hands are yours and conclusions marked by sighs and breathing. You are nowhere, a signal or code meant to sweep you under a wave or a cloud or a whispered veil of induction. The French Revolution began without you and ended the same. You are not needed in this chapter in which the king's clothes are described as raiment or ermine cloak. If you are required by time and its minions, you will receive notice, as spiders when the dew shakes a web and the world blinks to attention.

Followed and noticed, referenced and catalogued, perfection's garden posits its signs, in service to
its acacia, loam, and dark earth beneath the milked aspens. Reentering is justice, recompense, travelers
asleep with their conclusions. Aesthetics of want and labor, error and hope, wish and indifference face a
more distant north. You bear translations of snow, recite prophecies of smoke, exhale all visible means of
navigation beneath bright gestures. Where is your sign and your treason, your cape and your betrayal, your
measure, ancient and smoother than truth? Day-blind, sleep-neared, tucked in fog, you recede as myth of
birds' tender migration.

Time and its "It was."
—HEIDEGGER

You are not alone in the catalogue, you with your hourglass and omens, your presumptions and solos. You are a catacomb, black letters on dark stone, a series of hereafters punctuated by night's late pillow.

Another you waits like a pair of shoes on a staircase. Nothing wears its history darker than a purse of midnight, winter's hedge, astronomy's fictions. Orbit unknown, principles tossed by gravity, you are your own island, your own Egypt, speckled egg in a nest of gray feathers. Eyes attuned to life's curses and wax, its devotions and triptychs of blame. Glass stained and ripened by moonlight inscribed as thus, 'a pearly veil welcomes you, traveler.'

The muse of forgetfulness meets the muse of forgetting on an afternoon road. They wander together until a lamp intervenes and the scene is erased.

Late December's dimness lifts the green toward sky's smooth paper. The world is a camera. Words tie you to sparrows fence-colored in gardens of nothing past its season. Evening is a charm, its gold-threaded ending lost in the story.

Sustain patterns of meaning.
—MARTINE BELLEN

Lake's deep notion of speech, uncanny
if vague, sundered and rendered by photo or brush,
sample of white noise grafted to singing
by location one calls a view; there is a glade
crowded with time and slow reason, anchored by sound
that lifts, canopies of light over trees' witnessing branches,
sky's lingering arrangement, luster and shine, origin
unknown; limbs break in small wind, unencumber themselves
of accidental leaves, pinecones' postlude covers soil;
it is not music when a voice speaks its phrase, not a gift
of a box with a name, not a notation; no one asks
how lips move, how ears understand small grief
or tender issue. Dominating the view,
hands and shapes of hands, blue and white flicker
of wing, slow breath of afternoon's inscription.

The political rejects beauty on the grounds that it is too powerful.

—ELAINE SCARRY

Rich in landing, birds' parted grace notes in curtained leaf-light
flatter an eye at evening when fairness isn't human
but a quality of design. The sky, the air, small pebbles underfoot
attuned to its signature, tonal shift in the weather
as a voice lifts beyond its slightly treasonous place in the garden
among slow-growing and darkly ancient moss that welcomes north.
She is strange here on the page of sky, cloud galleons sweeping
overhead, small birds dotting the sentences, the world
punctuating a beautiful or terror-filled enterprise in a briny season.
She walks into the house and takes her place
among the paper, yarn and tools of nature's absence. Nothing wears
her name as shockingly as love on a Thursday, ancient practice, unable
to recover its bearings before itself as any small waterfall in spring. Rocks
lining its progress are background, the place of glistening as real as any plan.

Sound exists only as it is going out of existence.

—WALTER J. ONG

Shadow's interest accounts for parenthetical lips. Your only face,
a kind one, known to control the alphabet in slow whispers and embarkation.
If anyone should hear raw notes sway like laundry fainting into light,
they'd fear that symmetry is lost, time of day undone. We offer voices
which restore not much. In paradox we sing as freighters cross an ocean
and birds land on plastic flowers ripe with illusion. No audience
to witness its pitch of blue on Utopia Parkway, where he lived with boxes
and owls, wooden birds perched in present corners of attention. Who knows
what bridge will fall at seismic gasp, what world beyond all books and money.
History is emblem: we are lost in light that cannot fray and doesn't cost. No one to own
the horizon we create, the portal we carve of nothing on its way to itself and back again.

Years' tender operation, policies that love undrifts,
gaps of history fill with articles and pronouns,
sky's complacent beauty. What we value asks no limit:
gives rise to statements from a place of grief to holding,
unlike shells hold their only definition in briny water or a place beneath
a book, its cool reserve of wood and ruin. The quasi-plot involves
a pale, fog-lit street under lamps' discerning eye. Electricity cedes
to reference without pity or resolve. A hand opens on a stellar map
of skin, a face to certify the self and time, echo's fusion, seasons'
wheel of measure. In a multitude of times, stories themselves configure.

In sleep's vestibule shrines are lit
by due subtlety of staging.
You enter a hallway of illusion,
sceptered, adjudicated,
your value a length and a limit.
Globes present closure
as a golden chance, that which
shines toward you. You hold
as a planet might a brief eclipse or
as an alchemist, his signaled proof—
with an eye for justice,
an ear for clover on which a bee
has landed in figurative grace.
Tangled, over-determined,
shadows flicker, licensed, incensed
at their own complicity.
Nothing wears presence
as violet destination steeped

by reason's canny schedule
in sky's waning reference:
here are your oars, your sea,
your cargo of blossoming exceptions.

An affinity for string, ends dipped in bittersweet,
nestlings wrapped by sand funneling upwards.
She sees it at her ledge, where
wave and wave separate debris of living,
bottle cap, ledger, casement.
Kelp sign shoreline, installation
she has walked through.
Such silence in the tall bleached grass,
a hum of meaning of ears and hands,
project of being. Light enters its moment of repose,
strikes the wrong object, glass haphazardly lit,
wrong face poised for flattery or treason.
The purpose of time and its
interpretations, weightless as confetti,
falls on birds' wing, drifted wood,
wrist untangled thus. Life trumps life
in pity's ancient room.
Dust in a window empty as motive.
A stranger asks a question of sand and water,
and in response: birds' signatory presence.

The sunlight was of the same whiteness as your walls.
— BRADFORD MORROW

Your ceiling, tiled with feathers
of rare birds extinct in the catalogue,
your floor of lead and crystal where
feet never tread, eyes enter
the world, box of glitter and string
with shadows for meaning
in the windowed darkness—
who knows where the imagined
swan nests if, in late afternoon,
the willow near the rangy dogwood
bends toward the man who sits
in brackish grass, wondering
what *clothesline* means
in the century, new as surrender—
vacant letter, pale white sheet
on which sunlight tears
afternoon's watery prison
you are not a feature or reference,

not a windy ledger,
you are poison in the clover,
a takeoff and a landing
here, where I found you breathing

The path between us lifts,
under skies' notion of resolve
bottles lost at sea which float
like pearls in a dish under light
In a field of feathers
an owl has lifted its snowy head
and sought its prey
Would you feminize hunger
or allow pronouns to lose
their reference as bodies do
leaning into anchored sleep?

You are the one I took you for—
philosophy, language, air, and breath,
sublunar, beneath the shadow of eclipse,
under the stars' night of slow history
future and intention rest beneath
the story of doves' promised return

You are told in small degrees, you,
whose arm, hand, and fingerprint
are etched on glass, plotless
and verbless without your trace

Lost on a night when reference
suffices for human events,
the slow distance between bodies
reaches for narratives of innocence
or crushes as fallen feathers.
On a plank of sleep he sees the empty
tree, flown birds' narrow hotel
of blue and leaf and fragrant wood,
light, an envelope in her marble hand.
If reaching means proximity, life thinks
otherwise, leaves books open to weather,
pummels history with slow report. Explanations
slip as diamonds in a mossy sea, or time,
a science of feeling. Eclipse imminent,
papered walls suffer with impunity
the loss of probable light. We are not alone
with our discipline, the smooth stones we carve
from childhood to convergence to dawn.

Under the same photo of tree with its owl, dew with its feathers, light with its obstruction of motives, you name the moment by tying it to a stone, which itself has a history before yours and a future without you. Earthly life made of dirt and ashes, bones, and a cloistered devotion. Eyes blink until sleep's window parts shores. You bear witness to a dance that welcomes disclosure, as notes touch each other's edges. Subplot or subject, the story of an hour, ripeness seeks a lens to frame its arrival.

Calendars fill with lies. Who softens the day's bright ledger?
Posed in a room full of stillness, nothing drifts into view
but their shadows, gathered. It is the same as flying,
to drift in a vaporous sky. Nothing matches
its wispy guises, its tender undulations.
And you, dear eyes, pass as Venus did,
in a year of miracles, over the face of the sun.

Love's erasures tease out meaning
as blossoms thicken into carpet late that month.
Long and short breaths, a code of sums
uncalculated, a formula for Beatrice and weeds
mixed with woodbine, ink and lead. Alone in a room,
you stir limits and endings, seal words in wax,
tie up the curtain to let in the amber glow
of proper names. Here comes mortality,
as is its custom, undoing our best efforts
at insistence. A truce is observed in which the field
fills with recent weather and the proper bird
sings of Edens lost daily in the imperative of habit.
Undo my pieties, unhinge my last desires.
Let me lie down next to want, return as satisfied.

You harbor the scheme of language
broken in voicing. A shadow falls deeply
on the town's last door, hesitating as if to open
a proclivity for incompletion. Nothing gets witnessed
in the tongue of its birth. Nothing passes as idea
or omen. The orange in its rind, the core of the fruit
whose seeds are laid to rest without ceremony
among the plumage of birds and letters unsent.
You hold one in your hand, asking for clarity on a day
when eloquence is waste and silence an amulet.

There is a world in which the old tumult breathes its conclusions. Inside, we are purple notes and wings of doves, visibility nothing can equal, which holds us, hesitating, as if movement might break the tender chord we strike as antidote to time. Unmask me, double me, make me a tangent in your circle of radiant breath— here with you, where the said is an offering. We are reworked, the moment a measuring device and a grace note, sorrow's window closed to the view.

FLIGHT

The air grew stronger, the free spirit quivered for flight.

—THE HOUSE OF MIRTH

Consider the grove of birds, branch and pine:
the room they discover the summer
their hearts are full, no icons
or angels, no prophets
or stone to build what love
attends to as a hundred hearths
burning in one dreamed room.
To ask of oceans deep tendencies,
air's fitful communion outside
the window's dusky trees of summer
gauze and green winnowing below
the charted stars, articulation
of moon and intention.

Love's tender mercies clear the air,
unhinging the gate to practiced longing.
Tied to life, you spill into water, deeper
Than any atmosphere. Pastoral nature
Has no plastic flowers, no tragic exits,
No barges of machinery headed for
Kuala Lumpur. You are in it and
Of it, fleck of star, lip of tulip, smallest cleft
On the face of stone. Altering time
With your longing, you are erased
And redrawn with new eyes.

Redrawn with new eyes, longing erased by flower's machinery.

Nature's exit is time altered by intention, atmosphere absolute as a love letter.

Beyond the voice of language, nameless events tarnish their speaker,

depth a trick of eyes challenging mortal experience.

Too much to separate into the marvelous and its contrivances,

knowing how it feels to own grace, then lose its location.

Out of nature, out of time, sensed as a hunger for justice
or love. Richly ornamented as a mountain of lace or starkly withheld
as yesterday's greeting. It is not day when, eyes closed, you harvest
names. Paper offers its whiteness to your list of days.
Alone and counting, you reach the expectation of arrival,
borders crossed, windows open to the sudden day and its register of hours.
Someone says "session," as if to mean time enclosed by reason or want.
You reply without words. Speech is an act you must justify.
And then the rain comes, to alter the world's dull motifs.
Rest inside of language, love, surrendering intention.

Thorns contain the idea of failure.
Creation of mold and blackened
leaves, earth's coffin closes out wanting.
Never a ransom of speech near
a border, tender line of breath and hunger.
You speak of objects as needs,
as issue of having lost your swans.
Pockets empty you fill them
with measured desire, feeding
the birds your store of hours
on this small island you name
by standing in the gathering night,
presence paler than spilled moonlight,
filling the gaps with day's symmetry.

Dust enters dust in

motes of sheer light;

collapsing verbs meet

their careworn predicates.

The body's convictions

gesture at fluency,

absorbed as fruit

by the afternoon sun.

On a shoal above brackish

water and the hum

of heated air, you were

a detail, in the eyes

of thereafter. Come

to the window, where a heron

landed in the marsh grass

the summer you believed

that nothing his smooth voice

touched was lost in description.

to divide and to bring closer
—JOHN TAGGERT

Named trees witness an eternal present

above their faces, each earlobe memorized,

each curve their hemisphere made whole.

Darkness undresses the intermittent wind,

tearing the story's future: each loved object

a voice in the leaves, tender and green as its motives.

I would be a lamp for its passage from illusion,

the story lifting itself above the telling,

desire an accretion of love's present tense,

each word a bridge to the next erasure.

Shadowed and screened,

your place in the setting

is morning's task.

You ask the cortex

to light upon

a fly's buzzing as

interruption in the song

of recurrence. In a room

of simplifications, figure

and ground are disclosure,

the shapes at the window

a way of knowing.

Any clear pane reflects

sight and inclination.

You stand witnessing

the world's traffic,

words like any others

shaping a new

declension of need.

In certainty the self addresses longing, opens doors

to categories untouched by any leaf. Straining toward a shore

memories are erased as lessons in frugality. Nothing flies overhead

or calls for a voice beyond its range. No one comes to greet

the boat untethered at the shoreline, which takes on water and

glistens to no eye/ Nowhere offers its bells and charms

in banquets of forgetting. You opened a book as he sat reading.

The moment took on its irreducible claim to being when he

said a word you hastened to recall. At the edge of grief

the self required a table, a cup, a window overlooking the view,

a chance rare as green days in winter's interstices,

infinitude of meaning, whispered near the stairs.

White-winged clouds
will weave a shroud
for winter,
hyacinth unburied
from a bed of grey
beyond the fence.
Where he is, wind's
a factor, gray-lit
compromise of days
and calendars'
blown pages. Words
wear finer clothes.
Vernal equinox will split
the globe and mend
its green, loose yarns,
ball of air inside
a nest of string.

The book of dust
speaks of
the infinitesimal,
green dust
on fern fronds,
scattered light
of a candle,
flickering
in dappled light,
bodies, gathered
in sunlight,
an afternoon
bed whose seam
is the work
of being,
how, when
you turned to me,
your eyes suggested

personal economies
known beyond words.
Trapped in time
this story
nods to the future,
whose past still
reflects how
the gold beaters
and silver
threaders of
ancient Florence
would have paused
in their work
to notice our eyes,
incandescent,
as we passed
under their window.

We're younger than we ever were.

—JAMES SCHUYLER

Afternoon's bright awning
flashes violet in the newsy air.
If delight has a prince, we are
princes and thieves, grave
robbers and pirates on April
Fools' Eve when minor
characters gather at midnight
rehearsing their old roles,
translating all grievance until
the Milky Way unveils a new
world order. When the sky
lightens there will be folly,
dumb show, call and response,
a chorus of well-wishers
waking in each other's arms.

Beadworked cloth and peonies
in season tangle with the view
of Cezanne's apples and the glassy-eyed
hares, two centuries older
than the smoothness of the air,
who, wide-eyed, seem surprised by death.
Light asks questions, woven in
the story of afternoon's encounter
with rooms where martyrs flee
the scene of their demise.
You have stood where he is,
in his eyes a different light replete
with grace. His face supplants
the view. You see the rooms inside
the blueness of his eyes, another
sight of doves in white winged
wakefulness, a certain wanting
goes unanswered as stories when

they end leave permanence and sorrow.
There is comfort in the windowpanes'
dead stare of evening as you flee the frame.

The bend of grass

under sky's dim cloak

as eyes encounter

magnolias which mean

May though ice

lingers and the crocus

comes and goes,

as life remembers

its trance-like path

back to itself.